:andard Grade | Credit

Mathematics

Credit Level "1998"

Credit Level Model Paper 1
(based on 1998 exam)
Credit Level Model Paper 2
(based on 1998 exam)

Credit Level "1999"

Credit Level Model Paper 1
(based on 1999 exam)
Credit Level Model Paper 2
(based on 1999 exam)

Credit Level "2000"

Credit Level Model Paper 1
(based on 2000 exam)
Credit Level Model Paper 2
(based on 2000 exam)

Credit Level 2001

Credit Level 2001 Paper 1
Credit Level 2001 Paper 2

Credit Level 2002

Credit Level 2002 Paper 1
Credit Level 2002 Paper 2

Credit Level 2003

Credit Level 2003 Paper 1
Credit Level 2003 Paper 2

© Scottish Qualifications Authority

All rights reserved. Copying prohibited. No part of this publication may be reproduced, stored in a retrieval system, or transmitted in any form or by any means, electronic, mechanical, photocopying, recording or otherwise.

First exam published in 2001.
Published by
Leckie & Leckie, 8 Whitehill Terrace, St. Andrews, Scotland KY16 8RN
tel: 01334 475656 fax: 01334 477392
enquiries@leckieandleckie.co.uk www.leckieandleckie.co.uk

Leckie & Leckie Project Team: Peter Dennis; John MacPherson; Bruce Ryan; Andrea Smith

ISBN 1-84372-101-5

A CIP Catalogue record for this book is available from the British Library.

Printed in Scotland by Scotprint.

Leckie & Leckie is a division of Granada Learning Limited, part of Granada plc.

Scotland's leading educational publishers

Introduction

Dear Student,

This past paper book offers you the perfect opportunity to put into practice what you should know in order to do well in your exams. As these questions have actually appeared in the exam in previous years, you can be sure they reflect the kind of questions you will be asked this summer.

Work carefully through the papers, not only to test your knowledge and understanding but also your ability to handle information and work through more thought-provoking questions. Remember that you may not use a calculator for Paper 1. Use the answer booklet at the back of the book to check that you know exactly what the examiner is looking for to gain top marks. You will be able to focus on areas of weakness to sharpen your grasp of the subject and our top tips for revision and sitting the exam will also help to improve your performance on the day.

Remember, practice makes perfect! These past papers will show you what to expect in your exam, help to boost your confidence and feel ready to gain the grade you really want.

Good luck!

Acknowledgements

Every effort has been made to trace the copyright holders and to obtain their permission for the use of copyright material. Leckie & Leckie will gladly receive information enabling them to rectify any error or omission in subsequent editions.

1998 CREDIT

C

2500/405

NATIONAL
QUALIFICATIONS

Time: 45 minutes

BASED on the 1998 Question Paper

Due to the changes in format and syllabus
of the current paper, some amendments have
been made to the original paper.

MATHEMATICS
STANDARD GRADE
Credit Level
Paper 1
(Non-calculator)

1 **You may NOT use a calculator.**

2 Answer as many questions as you can.

3 Full credit will be given only where the solution contains appropriate working.

4 Square-ruled paper is provided.

SCOTTISH
QUALIFICATIONS
AUTHORITY

FORMULAE LIST

The roots of $ax^2 + bx + c = 0$ are $x = \dfrac{-b \pm \sqrt{(b^2 - 4ac)}}{2a}$

Sine rule: $\dfrac{a}{\sin A} = \dfrac{b}{\sin B} = \dfrac{c}{\sin C}$

Cosine rule: $a^2 = b^2 + c^2 - 2bc \cos A$ or $\cos A = \dfrac{b^2 + c^2 - a^2}{2bc}$

Area of a triangle: Area $= \frac{1}{2}ab \sin C$

Standard deviation: $s = \sqrt{\dfrac{\sum(x - \bar{x})^2}{n - 1}} = \sqrt{\dfrac{\sum x^2 - (\sum x)^2 / n}{n - 1}}$, where n is the sample size.

KU | RE

1. Evaluate

$$3{\cdot}3 - 2{\cdot}8 \times 0{\cdot}5.$$

2

2. Evaluate $a^2 + 2ab$ where $a = -5$ and $b = -4$.

2

3. $f(x) = \dfrac{3}{x^2}$

Find $f\left(\dfrac{1}{3}\right)$

2

4. A sequence of terms, starting with 1, is

1, 5, 9, 13, 17, ...

Consecutive terms in this sequence are formed by adding 4 to the previous term.

The total of consecutive terms of this sequence can be found using the following pattern.

Total of the first 2 terms: $1 + 5$ $= 2 \times 3$
Total of the first 3 terms: $1 + 5 + 9$ $= 3 \times 5$
Total of the first 4 terms: $1 + 5 + 9 + 13$ $= 4 \times 7$
Total of the first 5 terms: $1 + 5 + 9 + 13 + 17 = 5 \times 9$

(*a*) Express the total of the first 9 terms of this sequence in the same way.

2

(*b*) The first *n* terms of this sequence are added. Write down an expression, in *n*, for the total.

3

KU RE

5. Triangles ABE and ACD, with some of their measurements, are shown opposite.

Triangle ABE is similar to triangle ACD.

Calculate the length of BE.

Do not use a scale drawing.

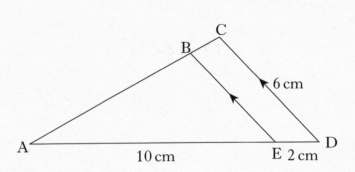

3

6. The following table shows the number of guests staying in a hotel and the number of nights each has booked.

Number of Nights	Number of Guests
1	33
2	17
3	9
4	8
5	3

(a) Construct a cumulative frequency column for this table.

1

(b) Calculate the median and the semi-interquartile range for the guests' length of stay.

3

KU | RE

7. The cost of taking a school group to the theatre can be calculated from the information shown below.

* 1 adult goes free for every 10 pupils *

Number of pupils	Cost per pupil	Cost per paying adult
less than 10	£5·00	£8·00
10 to 19	£4·50	£7·00
20 to 29	£4·00	£6·00
30 to 39	£3·00	£5·00

(a) Find the cost for a group of 12 pupils and 3 adults. 　　2

(b) Write down a formula to find the cost, £C, of taking a group of p pupils and d adults where $20 \leq p \leq 29$. 　　4

8. (a) Factorise $4a^2 - 9b^2$. 　　2

(b) Express as a single fraction in its simplest form

$$\frac{1}{2x} - \frac{1}{3x}, \quad x \neq 0.$$ 　　2

(c) Solve, **algebraically**, the equation

$$x^2 = 7x.$$ 　　3

9. (a) Multiply out the brackets

$$\sqrt{2}(\sqrt{6} - \sqrt{2}).$$

Express your answer as a **surd** in its simplest form. 　　2

(b) Express $\dfrac{b^{\frac{1}{2}} \times b^{\frac{3}{2}}}{b}$ in its simplest form. 　　2

[END OF QUESTION PAPER]

[BLANK PAGE]

C

2500/406

NATIONAL
QUALIFICATIONS

Time: 1 hour 20 minutes

BASED on the 1998 Question Paper

Due to the changes in format and syllabus
of the current paper, some amendments have
been made to the original paper.

MATHEMATICS
STANDARD GRADE
Credit Level
Paper 2

1 **You may use a calculator**.

2 Answer as many questions as you can.

3 Full credit will be given only where the solution contains appropriate working.

4 Square-ruled paper is provided.

SCOTTISH
QUALIFICATIONS
AUTHORITY
©

FORMULAE LIST

The roots of $ax^2 + bx + c = 0$ are $x = \dfrac{-b \pm \sqrt{(b^2 - 4ac)}}{2a}$

Sine rule: $\dfrac{a}{\sin A} = \dfrac{b}{\sin B} = \dfrac{c}{\sin C}$

Cosine rule: $a^2 = b^2 + c^2 - 2bc \cos A$ or $\cos A = \dfrac{b^2 + c^2 - a^2}{2bc}$

Area of a triangle: Area $= \frac{1}{2}ab \sin C$

Standard deviation: $s = \sqrt{\dfrac{\sum(x - \bar{x})^2}{n-1}} = \sqrt{\dfrac{\sum x^2 - (\sum x)^2 / n}{n-1}}$, where n is the sample size.

Page two

KU | RE

1. The annual profit (£) of a company was 3.2×10^9 for the year 1997.

   What profit did the company make per second?

   Give your answer to **three significant figures**.

   2

2. A skip is prism shaped as shown in figure 1.

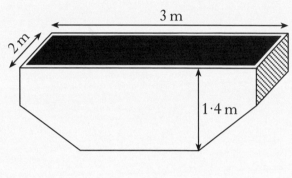

figure 1

The cross-section of the skip, with measurements in metres, is shown in figure 2.

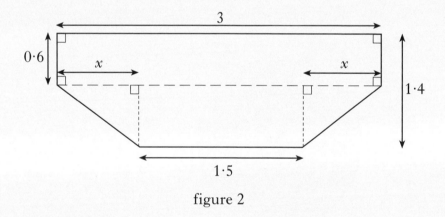

figure 2

(a) Find the value of x.

1

(b) Find the volume of the skip in cubic metres.

3

KU | RE

3. The diagram below shows a ceiling in the shape of a rectangle and a segment of a circle.

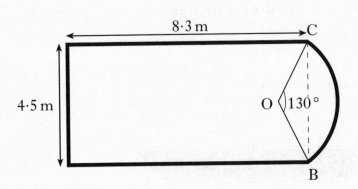

The rectangle measures 8·3 metres by 4·5 metres.

OB and OC are radii of the circle and angle BOC is 130°.

(*a*) Find the length of OB.

3

A border has to be fitted round the perimeter of the ceiling.

(*b*) Find the length of border required.

4

4. Figure 1 shows the circular cross-section of a tunnel with a horizontal floor.

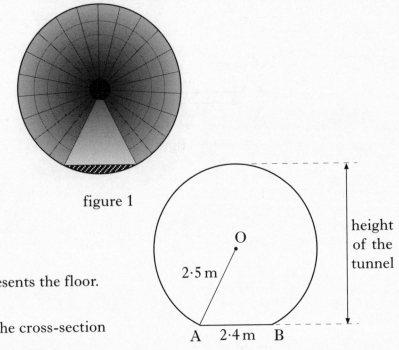

figure 1

In figure 2, AB represents the floor.
AB is 2·4 metres.

The radius, OA, of the cross-section is 2·5 metres.

Find the height of the tunnel.

figure 2

4

KU | RE

5. (*a*) Two dice are rolled simultaneously.

Find the probability that the total score will be greater than 10.

1

(*b*) If the two dice were rolled 300 times, how many times would you expect to see a total greater than 10?

1

One of the activities at a charity fund-raising event involves rolling two dice.

(*c*) The cost of one throw of the two dice is 50p.

The prize for scoring more than 10 is £1.

How much profit is the game likely to make if 300 people each have one turn?

2

6. An aeroplane is flying parallel to the ground.

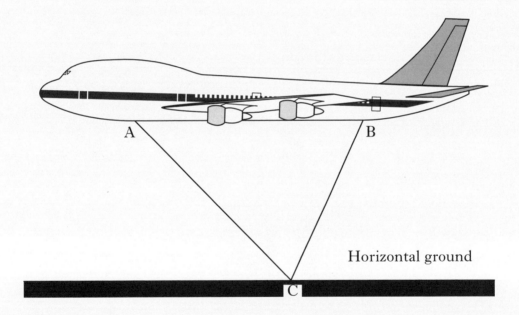

Horizontal ground

Lights have been fitted at A and B as shown in the diagram.

When the aeroplane is flying at a certain height, the beams from these lights meet exactly on the ground at C.

The angle of depression of the beam of light from A to C is 50°.

The angle of depression of the beam of light from B to C is 70°.

The distance AB is 20 metres.

Find the height of the aeroplane above C.

6

	KU	R

7. Solve, **algebraically**, the equation

$$7\cos x° - 2 = 0, \quad \text{for } 0 \le x < 360.$$

KU: 3

8. The time, T minutes, taken for a stadium to empty varies directly as the number of spectators, S, and inversely as the number of open exits, E.

   (a) Write down a relationship connecting T, S and E.

   KU: 1

   It takes 12 minutes for a stadium to empty when there are 20 000 spectators and 20 open exits.

   (b) How long does it take the stadium to empty when there are 36 000 spectators and 24 open exits?

   KU: 3

9. Traffic authorities are investigating the number of cars travelling along a busy stretch of road.

   They assume that all cars are travelling at a speed of v metres per second.

   The number of cars, N, which pass a particular point on the road in one minute is given by the formula

   $$N = \frac{30v}{2+v}.$$

   In one minute, 26 cars pass a point on the road.

   Find the speed of the cars in metres per second.

   R: 3

10. On a certain day the depth, D metres, of water at a fishing port, t hours after midnight, is given by the formula

   $$D = 12 \cdot 5 + 9 \cdot 5 \sin (30t)°.$$

   (a) Find the depth of the water at 1.30 pm.

   R: 3

   (b) The depth of water in the harbour is recorded each hour. What is the maximum difference in the depths of water in the harbour over the 24 hour period?

   Show clearly all your working.

   R: 3

KU | RE

8. A mini lottery game uses **red**, **green**, **blue** and **yellow** balls.

There are 10 of **each** colour, numbered from 1 to 10.

The balls are placed in a drum and one is drawn out.

(a) What is the probability that it is a **6**?

1

(b) What is the probability that it is a **yellow 6**?

1

9. A random check is carried out on the contents of a number of matchboxes.

A summary of the results is shown in the boxplot below.

47   50   51   53   54

What percentage of matchboxes contains fewer than 50 matches?

1

10. School theatre visits are arranged for parents, teachers and pupils.

The ratio of parents to teachers to pupils **must** be 1 : 3 : 15.

(a) 45 pupils want to go to the theatre.

How many teachers must accompany them?

1

(b) The theatre gives the school 100 tickets for a play.

What is the maximum number of pupils who can go to the play?

3

[Turn over

KU | RE

11. Using the sequence

$$1, \ 3, \ 5, \ 7, \ 9, \ldots$$

    (a) Find S_3, the sum of the first 3 numbers.

1

    (b) Find S_n, the sum of the first n numbers.

2

    (c) Hence or otherwise, find the $(n + 1)^{th}$ term of the sequence.

2

12. (a) Evaluate

$$8^{\frac{2}{3}}.$$

2

    (b) Simplify

$$\frac{\sqrt{24}}{\sqrt{2}}.$$

2

KU | RE

11. A 3 × 3 square has been identified on the calendar below.

The numbers in the diagonally opposite corners of the square are multiplied. These products are then subtracted in the order shown below.

$$(23 \times 11) - (25 \times 9) = 28$$

M	T	W	T	F	S	S
		1	2	3	4	5
6	7	8	9	10	11	12
13	14	15	16	17	18	19
20	21	22	23	24	25	26
27	28	29	30	31		

(a) Repeat the above process for a different 3 × 3 square.

Show clearly all your working.

1

(b) Prove that **in every** 3 × 3 square on the calendar above the process gives the answer 28.

3

[END OF QUESTION PAPER]

1999 CREDIT

C

2500/405

NATIONAL
QUALIFICATIONS

Time: 45 minutes

BASED on the 1999 Question Paper

Due to the changes in format and syllabus
of the current paper, some amendments have
been made to the original paper.

MATHEMATICS
STANDARD GRADE
Credit Level
Paper 1
(Non-calculator)

1 **You may NOT use a calculator**.

2 Answer as many questions as you can.

3 Full credit will be given only where the solution contains appropriate working.

4 Square-ruled paper is provided.

SCOTTISH
QUALIFICATIONS
AUTHORITY

©

FORMULAE LIST

The roots of $ax^2 + bx + c = 0$ are $x = \dfrac{-b \pm \sqrt{(b^2 - 4ac)}}{2a}$

Sine rule: $\dfrac{a}{\sin A} = \dfrac{b}{\sin B} = \dfrac{c}{\sin C}$

Cosine rule: $a^2 = b^2 + c^2 - 2bc \cos A$ or $\cos A = \dfrac{b^2 + c^2 - a^2}{2bc}$

Area of a triangle: Area $= \frac{1}{2}ab \sin C$

Standard deviation: $s = \sqrt{\dfrac{\sum(x - \bar{x})^2}{n-1}} = \sqrt{\dfrac{\sum x^2 - (\sum x)^2 / n}{n-1}}$, where n is the sample size.

	KU	RE

1. Evaluate

$$3 \times 1{\cdot}5 - 0{\cdot}8 \div 2.$$

2. Evaluate

$$20 - 4x^2y \text{ where } x = -1 \text{ and } y = 3.$$

3. Evaluate

$$3\frac{1}{5} - \frac{2}{3}.$$

4. Factorise $3x^2 - 5x - 2$.

5. The following stem-and-leaf diagram shows the number of words in a sample of 50 sentences selected from Sir Walter Scott's novel Ivanhoe.

Length of sentences

0	79
1	0001111223444
1	5555566788
2	011134
2	5566778
3	0111234
3	578
4	04

$n = 50$ 4 | 0 represents 40 words

(a) Write down the median length of a sentence in this sample.

(b) Draw another appropriate statistical diagram to illustrate the above information.

KU values: 2, 2, 2, 2, 1
RE values: 4

KU R

6.

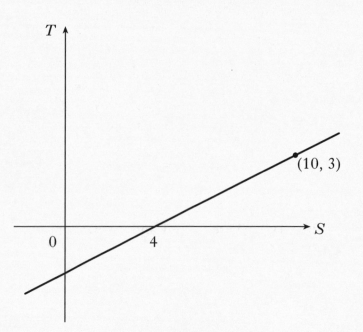

Find the equation of the given straight line in terms of T and S.   4

7.

The tickets for a Sports Club disco cost £2 for members and £3 for non-members.

(*a*) The total ticket money collected was £580.

    x tickets were sold to members and y tickets were sold to non-members.

    Use this information to write down an equation involving x and y.   2

(*b*) 250 people bought tickets for the disco.

    Write down another equation involving x and y.   1

(*c*) How many tickets were sold to members?   3

KU | RE

8.

> A Fibonacci sequence is a sequence of numbers.
>
> After the first two terms, each term is the sum of the previous two terms.
>
>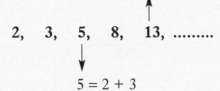
>
> eg   2,   3,   5,   8,   13, ...

(a) Write down the next three terms of this Fibonacci sequence.

$$5, \quad -1, \quad 4, \underline{\quad}, \underline{\quad}, \underline{\quad},$$

1

(b) For the Fibonacci sequence

$$4, \quad -3, \quad 1, \quad -2, \quad -1, \quad -3, \quad -4, \quad ....$$

show that the sum of the first six terms is equal to four times the fifth term.

2

(c) If p and q are the first two terms of a Fibonacci sequence, **prove** that the sum of the first six terms is equal to four times the fifth term.

3

9. Solve **algebraically** the inequality

$$5x - 4 < 2(1 - 2x).$$

3

10. $f(x) = 3^x$

(a) Find $f(4)$.

1

(b) Given that $f(x) = \sqrt{27}$, find x.

3

[END OF QUESTION PAPER]

C

2500/406

NATIONAL
QUALIFICATIONS

Time: 1 hour 20 minutes

BASED on the 1999 Question Paper

Due to the changes in format and syllabus
of the current paper, some amendments have
been made to the original paper.

MATHEMATICS
STANDARD GRADE
Credit Level
Paper 2

1 **You may use a calculator**.

2 Answer as many questions as you can.

3 Full credit will be given only where the solution contains appropriate working.

4 Square-ruled paper is provided.

SCOTTISH
QUALIFICATIONS
AUTHORITY
©

FORMULAE LIST

The roots of $ax^2 + bx + c = 0$ are $x = \dfrac{-b \pm \sqrt{(b^2 - 4ac)}}{2a}$

Sine rule: $\dfrac{a}{\sin A} = \dfrac{b}{\sin B} = \dfrac{c}{\sin C}$

Cosine rule: $a^2 = b^2 + c^2 - 2bc \cos A$ or $\cos A = \dfrac{b^2 + c^2 - a^2}{2bc}$

Area of a triangle: Area $= \frac{1}{2}ab \sin C$

Standard deviation: $s = \sqrt{\dfrac{\sum(x - \bar{x})^2}{n-1}} = \sqrt{\dfrac{\sum x^2 - (\sum x)^2 / n}{n-1}}$, where n is the sample size.

KU | RE

1. Paul bought a car last year.

It has lost $12\frac{1}{2}\%$ of its value since then.

It is now valued at £10 500.

How much did Paul pay for his car?

2

2. A newspaper report stated:

"Concorde has now flown $7 \cdot 1 \times 10^7$ miles.

This is equivalent to 300 journeys from the earth to the moon."

Calculate the distance from the earth to the moon.

Give your answer in **scientific notation correct to 2 significant figures**.

3

3. The diagram shows the positions of a helicopter base and two oil rigs, Delta and Gamma.

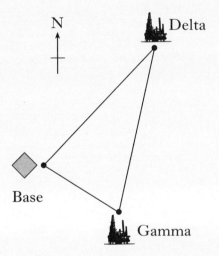

From the helicopter base, the oil rig Delta is 35 kilometres away on a bearing of 050°.

From the same base, the oil rig Gamma is 20 kilometres away on a bearing of 125°.

Calculate the distance between Delta and Gamma.

Do not use a scale drawing.

5

KU | R

4. The blood pressure of a sample of 9 young women was measured in mm.

The data gave the following summary totals:

$$\sum x = 1156 \text{ and } \sum x^2 = 148980$$

(a) Calculate the sample mean and standard deviation, giving your answers correct to 1 decimal place.

3

(b) A group of older women had a mean blood pressure of 158·0 mm and a standard deviation of 8·6 mm. How does the blood pressure of these older women compare with that of the younger women?

2

5. Solve **algebraically** the equation

$$2 + 3\sin x° = 0 \text{ for } 0 \le x < 360.$$

3

6. The diagram shows a table whose top is in the shape of part of a circle with centre, O, and radius 60 centimetres.

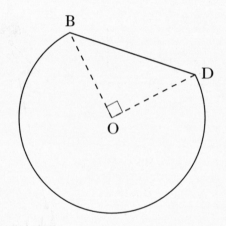

BD is a straight line.

Angle BOD is 90°.

Calculate the perimeter of the table top.

3

KU | RE

7. A wooden toy box is prism-shaped as shown in figure 1.

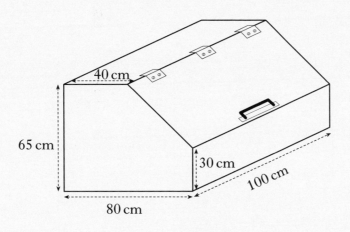

figure 1

The uniform cross-section of the box is shown in figure 2.

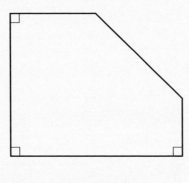

figure 2

Calculate the volume of the box in **cubic metres**.

4

8. The diagram below shows two jugs which are mathematically similar.

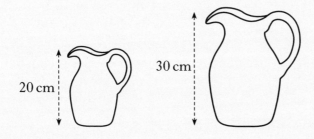

The volume of the smaller jug is 0·8 litre.

Find the volume of the larger jug.

3

KU | RE

9. The end wall of a bungalow is in the shape of a rectangle and a triangle as shown below.

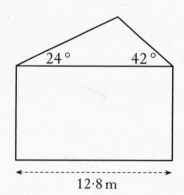

The roof has one edge inclined at 24° to the horizontal and the other edge inclined at 42° to the horizontal.

The width of the house is 12·8 metres.

Calculate the length of the longer sloping edge of the roof.

Do not use a scale drawing.

4

10. A statue stands at the corner of a square courtyard.

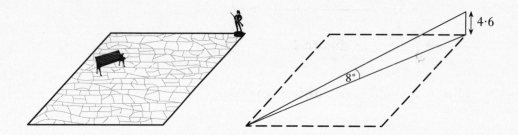

The statue is 4·6 metres high.

The angle of elevation from the opposite corner of the courtyard to the top of the statute is 8°.

(a) Find the distance from the base of the statue to the opposite corner of the courtyard.

2

(b) Show that the length of the side of the courtyard is approximately 23 metres.

3

KU | RE

11.

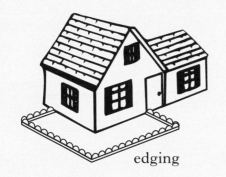

A gardener creates an L-shaped flower-bed. He uses the house walls and concrete edging for the boundary as shown in figure 1.

edging

figure 1

He plans his flower-bed as shown in figure 2.

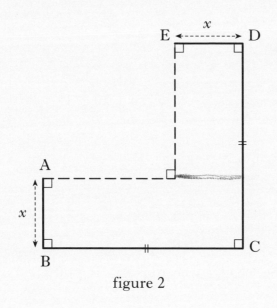

figure 2

(a) He uses a total of **6 metres of edging**.

$AB = ED = x$ metres
$BC = DC$

Show that the length, in metres, of BC can be expressed as $BC = 3 - x$.

2

(b) Hence show that the area, A, in square metres, of the flower-bed can be expressed as

$$A = 6x - 3x^2.$$

3

(c) Calculate **algebraically** the maximum area of the flower-bed.

3

KU | RE

12.

The table below shows the distances, in metres (d), travelled by a snowboarder in seconds (t).

Time in seconds (t)	1	2	3	4
Distance in metres (d)	5	20	45	80

(a) Explain why d varies directly as t^2.

1

(b) Write down the formula connecting d and t.

1

(c) How does the distance change when the time is multiplied by six?

2

[END OF QUESTION PAPER]

2000 CREDIT

C

2500/405

NATIONAL
QUALIFICATIONS

Time: 45 minutes

BASED on the 2000 Question Paper

Due to the changes in format and syllabus of the current paper, some amendments have been made to the original paper.

MATHEMATICS
STANDARD GRADE
Credit Level
Paper 1
(Non-calculator)

1 **You may NOT use a calculator**.

2 Answer as many questions as you can.

3 Full credit will be given only where the solution contains appropriate working.

4 Square-ruled paper is provided.

FORMULAE LIST

The roots of $ax^2 + bx + c = 0$ are $x = \dfrac{-b \pm \sqrt{(b^2 - 4ac)}}{2a}$

Sine rule: $\dfrac{a}{\sin A} = \dfrac{b}{\sin B} = \dfrac{c}{\sin C}$

Cosine rule: $a^2 = b^2 + c^2 - 2bc \cos A$ or $\cos A = \dfrac{b^2 + c^2 - a^2}{2bc}$

Area of a triangle: Area $= \frac{1}{2}ab \sin C$

Standard deviation: $s = \sqrt{\dfrac{\sum(x - \bar{x})^2}{n-1}} = \sqrt{\dfrac{\sum x^2 - (\sum x)^2 / n}{n-1}}$, where n is the sample size.

	KU	RE

1. Evaluate

$$18 - 12{\cdot}5 \div 5.$$

KU **2**

2. Evaluate

$$\frac{2}{7} \text{ of } \left(\frac{1}{3} + \frac{1}{4} \right).$$

KU **2**

3. $f(x) = 2x - 5x^2$.

Find $f(-2)$.

KU **2**

4. (*a*) Factorise $x^2 - 16$.

KU **1**

(*b*) Express $\dfrac{5(2x - 3)}{4x^2 - 9}$ in its simplest form.

KU **2**

5. Fifty people took part in a Health Promotion Campaign. They were asked whether or not they smoked cigarettes. The following table summarises the responses.

	Smoker	Non Smoker
Male	3	21
Female	8	18

What is the probability that a person chosen at random from this group is

(*a*) male;

KU **1**

(*b*) a smoker;

KU **1**

(*c*) a female who smokes?

KU **1**

KU RI

6.

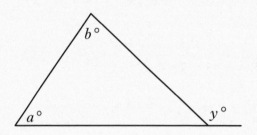

Use the information in the above diagram to find a relationship connecting a, b and y.

2

7. Jamie conducted a survey.

He asked his classmates how they had travelled to school that day.

Here are their replies:

Walk   13
Bus   9
Car   6
Cycle   2

Draw an appropriate statistical diagram to illustrate this information.

4

8. Solve **algebraically** the inequality

$$2y < 3 - (y + 6).$$

3

9. (*a*) Remove the brackets and simplify

$$a^{\frac{1}{2}}\left(a + \frac{1}{a}\right).$$

2

(*b*) Express $\sqrt{18} - \sqrt{2}$ as a surd in its simplest form.

2

KU | RE

10. The tank of a car contains 5 litres of petrol.

The graph below shows how the volume of petrol in this tank changes as a further 45 litres of petrol is pumped in at a steady rate for 60 seconds.

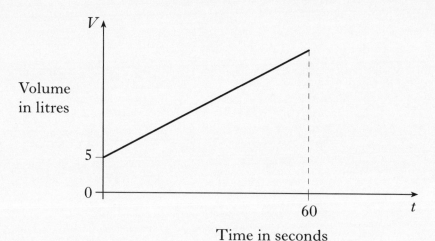

Find the equation of the straight line in terms of V and t.

4

11.   **1,   3,   5,   7,   ...**

The **first** odd number can be expressed as $1 = 1^2 - 0^2$.

The **second** odd number can be expressed as $3 = 2^2 - 1^2$.

The **third** odd number can be expressed as $5 = 3^2 - 2^2$.

(a) Express the **fourth** odd number in this form.

1

(b) Express the number 19 in this form.

1

(c) Write down a formula for the nth odd number and simplify this expression.

2

[*END OF QUESTION PAPER*]

C

2500/406

NATIONAL QUALIFICATIONS

Time: 1 hour 20 minutes

BASED on the 2000 Question Paper

Due to the changes in format and syllabus of the current paper, some amendments have been made to the original paper.

MATHEMATICS
STANDARD GRADE
Credit Level
Paper 2

1 **You may use a calculator**.

2 Answer as many questions as you can.

3 Full credit will be given only where the solution contains appropriate working.

4 Square-ruled paper is provided.

SCOTTISH
QUALIFICATIONS
AUTHORITY
©

FORMULAE LIST

The roots of $ax^2 + bx + c = 0$ are $x = \dfrac{-b \pm \sqrt{(b^2 - 4ac)}}{2a}$

Sine rule: $\dfrac{a}{\sin A} = \dfrac{b}{\sin B} = \dfrac{c}{\sin C}$

Cosine rule: $a^2 = b^2 + c^2 - 2bc \cos A$ or $\cos A = \dfrac{b^2 + c^2 - a^2}{2bc}$

Area of a triangle: Area $= \frac{1}{2}ab \sin C$

Standard deviation: $s = \sqrt{\dfrac{\sum(x - \bar{x})^2}{n - 1}} = \sqrt{\dfrac{\sum x^2 - (\sum x)^2 / n}{n - 1}}$, where n is the sample size.

KU | RE

1. In January 1999, it was estimated that the number of monkeys in a colony was 5000.

   The number of monkeys is decreasing at the rate of 12% per year.

   How many monkeys are expected to be in this colony in January 2002?

   Give your answer **to the nearest 10**.

   4

2. The mass of water on the earth's surface is $1 \cdot 41 \times 10^{18}$ tonnes.

   The total mass of the earth is $5 \cdot 97 \times 10^{21}$ tonnes.

   Express the mass of water on the earth's surface as a percentage of the total mass of the earth.

   Give your answer in **scientific notation**.

   3

3. Solve the equation $x^2 + 3x - 5 = 0$.

   Give your answer **correct to 2 significant figures**.

   4

4. The figures below show the total length, in mm, of a sample of 5 sparrows, captured during a bird ringing exercise.

   | 162 | 152 | 159 | 155 | 163 |

   Calculate the sample mean and standard deviation for these measurements, giving your answers correct to 1 decimal place.

   3

KU R

5.

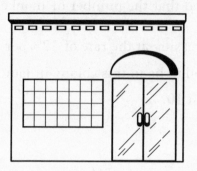

A rectangular window has length, l centimetres and breadth, b centimetres.

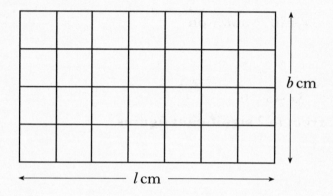

b cm

l cm

A security grid is made to fit this window. The grid has 5 horizontal wires and 8 vertical wires.

(a) The perimeter of the window is 260 centimetres.

Use this information to write down an equation involving l and b.   1

(b) In total, 770 centimetres of wire are used.

Write down another equation involving l and b.   2

(c) Find the length and breadth of the window.   3

6. Triangle ABC has an area of 14 square centimetres.

AB is 6 centimetres and AC is 7 centimetres.

Calculate the possible **sizes** of angle BAC.   4

KU | RE

7. A newspaper group advertises a new magazine on a helium balloon.

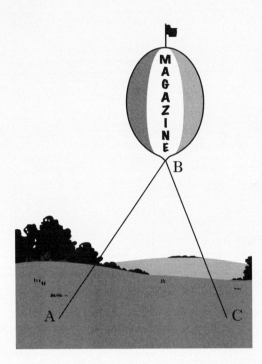

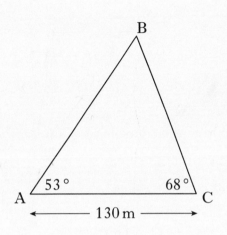

From the base of the balloon, B, two holding wires are attached to the ground at A and C.

The distance from A to C is 130 metres.

From A, the angle of elevation of B is 53°.

From C, the angle of elevation of B is 68°.

Calculate the height of point B above the ground.

Do not use a scale drawing.

5

KU | RE

8. A **rectangular** picture frame is to be made.

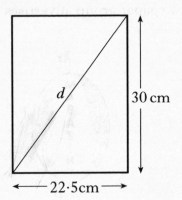

It is 30 centimetres high and 22·5 centimetres wide, as shown.

To check that the frame is rectangular, the diagonal, *d*, is measured.

It is 37·3 centimetres long.

Is the frame rectangular?

4

9. The height, *H* metres, of the tide-mark in a harbour is given by the formula

$$H = 14 + 3\cos(30n)°$$

where *n* is the number of hours after midnight.

(a) Find the height of the tide-mark at 2 am.

2

(b) When, after midnight, is the first time that the height of the tide-mark is 12·5 metres?

3

KU | RE

10. A glass vase, in the shape of a cuboid with a square base, is 20 centimetres high.

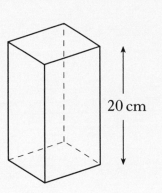

It is packed in a cardboard cylinder with radius 6 centimetres and height 20 centimetres.

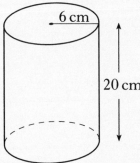

The corners of the vase touch the inside of the cylinder as shown.

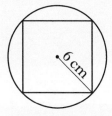

Show that the volume of the space between the vase and the cylinder is $720(\pi - 2)$ cubic centimetres.

5

KU | RE

11. A lampshade is made in the shape of a cone, as shown.

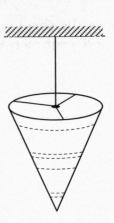

The shape of the material used for the lampshade is a sector of a circle.

The circle has radius 25 centimetres and the angle of the sector is 280°.

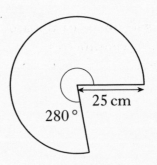

(a) Find the area of the sector of the circle.   3

Each sector is cut from a rectangular piece of material, 50 centimetres wide.

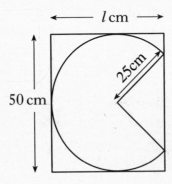

(b) Find, to the nearest centimetre, the **minimum** length, l, required for the piece of material.   4

[END OF QUESTION PAPER]

2001 CREDIT

C

2500/405

NATIONAL
QUALIFICATIONS
2001

WEDNESDAY, 16 MAY
1.30 PM – 2.25 PM

MATHEMATICS
STANDARD GRADE
Credit Level
Paper 1
(Non-calculator)

1 **You may NOT use a calculator**.

2 Answer as many questions as you can.

3 Full credit will be given only where the solution contains appropriate working.

4 Square-ruled paper is provided.

SCOTTISH
QUALIFICATIONS
AUTHORITY

FORMULAE LIST

The roots of $ax^2 + bx + c = 0$ are $x = \dfrac{-b \pm \sqrt{(b^2 - 4ac)}}{2a}$

Sine rule: $\dfrac{a}{\sin A} = \dfrac{b}{\sin B} = \dfrac{c}{\sin C}$

Cosine rule: $a^2 = b^2 + c^2 - 2bc \cos A$ or $\cos A = \dfrac{b^2 + c^2 - a^2}{2bc}$

Area of a triangle: $\text{Area} = \tfrac{1}{2}ab \sin C$

Volume of a cylinder: $\text{Volume} = \pi r^2 h$

Standard deviation: $s = \sqrt{\dfrac{\sum(x - \bar{x})^2}{n-1}} = \sqrt{\dfrac{\sum x^2 - (\sum x)^2 / n}{n-1}}$, where n is the sample size.

	KU	RE

1. Evaluate

$$3{\cdot}1 + 2{\cdot}6 \times 4.$$

[KU 2]

2. Evaluate

$$3\tfrac{5}{8} + 4\tfrac{2}{3}.$$

[KU 2]

3. Given that $f(m) = m^2 - 3m$, evaluate $f(-5)$.

[KU 2]

4. Solve **algebraically** the equation

$$2x - \frac{(3x-1)}{4} = 4.$$

[KU 3]

5. A furniture maker investigates the delivery times, in days, of two local wood companies and obtains the following data.

Company	Minimum	Maximum	Lower Quartile	Median	Upper Quartile
Timberplan	16	56	34	38	45
Allwoods	18	53	22	36	49

(a) Draw an appropriate statistical diagram to illustrate these two sets of data.

[RE 3]

(b) Given that consistency of delivery is the most important factor, which company should the furniture maker use? Give a reason for your answer.

[RE 1]

[Turn over

KU RE

6. A is the point (a^2, a).

T is the point (t^2, t), $a \neq t$

Find the gradient of the line AT.

Give your answer in its simplest form.

3

7. A garage carried out a survey on 600 cars.

The results are shown in the table below.

	Engine size (cc)			
	0–1000	1001–1500	1501–2000	2001+
Age Less than 3 years	50	80	160	20
3 years or more	60	100	120	10

(a) What is the probability that a car, chosen at random, is less than 3 years old?

1

(b) In a sample of 4200 cars, how many would be expected to have an engine size greater than 2000cc **and** be 3 or more years old?

2

KU RE

8. The diagram below shows part of the graph of $y = 4x^2 + 4x - 3$.

The graph cuts the y-axis at A and the x-axis at B and C.

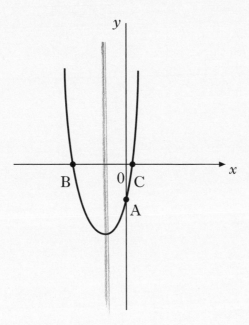

(a) Write down the coordinates of A.

1

(b) Find the coordinates of B and C.

3

(c) Calculate the minimum value of $4x^2 + 4x - 3$.

2

9. A number pattern is shown below.

$$1^3 + 1 = (1 + 1)(1^2 - 1 + 1)$$
$$2^3 + 1 = (2 + 1)(2^2 - 2 + 1)$$
$$3^3 + 1 = (3 + 1)(3^2 - 3 + 1)$$

(a) Write down a similar expression for $7^3 + 1$.

1

(b) Hence write down an expression for $n^3 + 1$.

1

(c) Hence find an expression for $8p^3 + 1$.

2

[Turn over

KU | RF

10. Simplify

$$\frac{\sqrt{3}}{\sqrt{24}}.$$

Express your answer as a fraction with a rational denominator.

3

11. The intensity of light, I, emerging after passing through a liquid with concentration, c, is given by the equation

$$I = \frac{20}{2^c} \qquad c \geq 0.$$

(a) Find the intensity of light when the concentration is 3.

1

(b) Find the concentration of the liquid when the intensity is 10.

2

(c) What is the maximum possible intensity?

3

[END OF QUESTION PAPER]

C

2500/406

NATIONAL
QUALIFICATIONS
2001

WEDNESDAY, 16 MAY
2.45 PM – 4.05 PM

MATHEMATICS
STANDARD GRADE
Credit Level
Paper 2

1 **You may use a calculator**.

2 Answer as many questions as you can.

3 Full credit will be given only where the solution contains appropriate working.

4 Square-ruled paper is provided.

SCOTTISH
QUALIFICATIONS
AUTHORITY

©

FORMULAE LIST

The roots of $ax^2 + bx + c = 0$ are $x = \dfrac{-b \pm \sqrt{(b^2 - 4ac)}}{2a}$

Sine rule: $\dfrac{a}{\sin A} = \dfrac{b}{\sin B} = \dfrac{c}{\sin C}$

Cosine rule: $a^2 = b^2 + c^2 - 2bc \cos A$ or $\cos A = \dfrac{b^2 + c^2 - a^2}{2bc}$

Area of a triangle: Area $= \frac{1}{2}ab \sin C$

Volume of a cylinder: Volume $= \pi r^2 h$

Standard deviation: $s = \sqrt{\dfrac{\sum(x - \bar{x})^2}{n-1}} = \sqrt{\dfrac{\sum x^2 - (\sum x)^2 / n}{n-1}}$, where n is the sample size.

KU | RE

1.

How many chocpops will be eaten in the year 2001?

Give your answer in **scientific notation**.

2

2. The price, in pence per litre, of petrol at 10 city garages is shown below.

84·2   84·4   85·1   83·9   81·0

84·2   85·6   85·2   84·9   84·8

(a) Calculate the mean and standard deviation of these prices.

3

(b) In 10 rural garages, the petrol prices had a mean of 88·8 and a standard deviation of 2·4.

How do the rural prices compare with the city prices?

2

3. In 1999, a house was valued at £90 000 and the contents were valued at £60 000.

The value of the house **appreciates** by 5% each year.

The value of the contents **depreciates** by 8% each year.

What will be the **total** value of the house **and** the contents in 2002?

3

[Turn over

KU | RE

4. A water pipe runs between two buildings.

   These are represented by the points A and B in the diagram below.

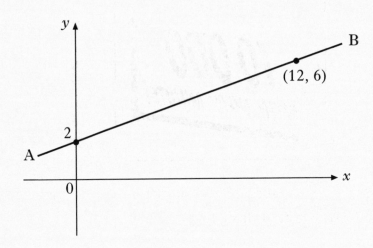

(a) Using the information in the diagram, show that the equation of the line AB is $3y - x = 6$.

3

(b) An emergency outlet pipe has to be built across the main pipe. The line representing this outlet pipe has equation $4y + 5x = 46$.

   Calculate the coordinates of the point on the diagram at which the outlet pipe will cut across the main water pipe.

4

5. A cylindrical soft drinks can is 15 centimetres in height and 6·5 centimetres in diameter.

   A new cylindrical can holds the same volume but has a reduced height of 12 centimetres.

   What is the diameter of the new can?

   Give your answer **to 1 decimal place**.

4

KU | RE

6. Three radio masts, Kangaroo (K), Wallaby (W) and Possum (P) are situated in the Australian outback.

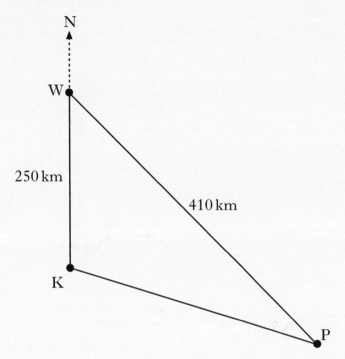

Kangaroo is 250 kilometres due south of Wallaby.

Wallaby is 410 kilometres from Possum.

Possum is on a bearing of 130° from Kangaroo.

Calculate the bearing of Possum from Wallaby.

Do not use a scale drawing.

4

7. Solve **algebraically** the equation

$$\tan 40° = 2\sin x° + 1 \qquad 0 \le x < 360.$$

3

[Turn over

KU RI

8. A metal door-stop is prism shaped, as shown.

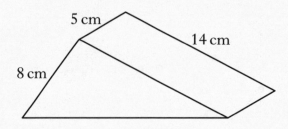

The uniform cross-section is shown below.

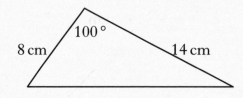

Find the volume of metal required to make the door-stop.

4

9. The electrical resistance, R, of copper wire varies directly as its length, L metres, and inversely as the square of its diameter, d millimetres.

Two lengths of copper wire, A and B, have the same resistance.

Wire A has a diameter of 2 millimetres and a length of 3 metres.

Wire B has a diameter of 3 millimetres.

What is the length of wire B?

4

KU | RE

10. Each leg of a folding table is prevented from opening too far by a metal bar.

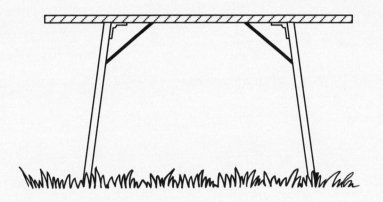

The metal bar is 21 centimetres long.

It is fixed to the table **top** 14 centimetres from the hinge and to the table **leg** 12 centimetres from the hinge.

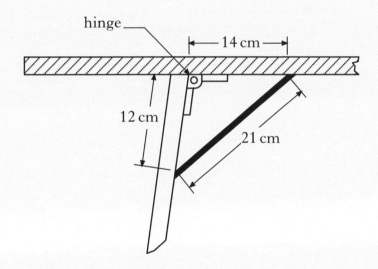

(a) Calculate the size of the obtuse angle which the table top makes with the leg.

3

(b) Given that the table leg is 70 centimetres long, calculate the height of the table.

3

[Turn over for Question 11 on *Page eight*

KU RK

11. A rectangular wall vent is 30 centimetres long and 20 centimetres wide.

It is to be enlarged by increasing **both** the length and the width by x centimetres.

(a) Write down the length of the new vent.

1

(b) Show that the area, A square centimetres, of the new vent is given by

$$A = x^2 + 50x + 600.$$

2

(c) The area of the new vent **must** be **at least** 40% more than the original area.

Find the **minimum** dimensions, to the nearest centimetre, of the new vent.

5

[END OF QUESTION PAPER]

2002 CREDIT

C

2500/405

| NATIONAL QUALIFICATIONS 2002 | THURSDAY, 9 MAY 1.30 PM – 2.25 PM | MATHEMATICS STANDARD GRADE Credit Level Paper 1 (Non-calculator) |

1 **You may NOT use a calculator**.

2 Answer as many questions as you can.

3 Full credit will be given only where the solution contains appropriate working.

4 Square-ruled paper is provided.

Scottish
Qualifications
Authority

LIB 2500/405 6/33570 ©

FORMULAE LIST

The roots of $ax^2 + bx + c = 0$ are $x = \dfrac{-b \pm \sqrt{(b^2 - 4ac)}}{2a}$

Sine rule: $\dfrac{a}{\sin A} = \dfrac{b}{\sin B} = \dfrac{c}{\sin C}$

Cosine rule: $a^2 = b^2 + c^2 - 2bc \cos A$ or $\cos A = \dfrac{b^2 + c^2 - a^2}{2bc}$

Area of a triangle: $\text{Area} = \frac{1}{2}ab \sin C$

Standard deviation: $s = \sqrt{\dfrac{\sum(x - \bar{x})^2}{n - 1}} = \sqrt{\dfrac{\sum x^2 - (\sum x)^2 / n}{n - 1}}$, where n is the sample size.

KU | RE

1. Evaluate
$$7 \cdot 18 - 2 \cdot 1 \times 3.$$

2

2. Evaluate
$$1\tfrac{1}{8} \div \tfrac{3}{4}.$$

2

3. Solve the inequality $5 - x > 2(x + 1)$.

3

4. Given that $f(x) = x^2 + 5x$, evaluate $f(-3)$.

2

5. (a) Factorise $p^2 - 4q^2$.

1

(b) Hence simplify
$$\frac{p^2 - 4q^2}{3p + 6q}.$$

2

6. $L = \tfrac{1}{2}(h - t)$.

Change the subject of the formula to h.

2

[Turn over

KU | RE

7. In triangle ABC,

AB = 4 units
AC = 5 units
BC = 6 units.

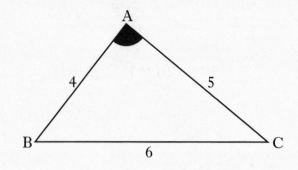

Show that $\cos A = \frac{1}{8}$.

3

8. Fifteen medical centres each **handed out** a questionnaire to fifty patients.

The numbers who replied to each centre are shown below.

| 11 | 19 | 22 | 25 | 25 |

| 29 | 31 | 34 | 36 | 38 |

| 40 | 46 | 49 | 50 | 50 |

Also, they each **posted** the questionnaire to another fifty patients.

The numbers who replied to each centre are shown below.

| 15 | 15 | 21 | 22 | 23 |

| 25 | 26 | 31 | 33 | 34 |

| 37 | 39 | 41 | 46 | 46 |

Draw an appropriate statistical diagram to compare these two sets of data.

3

9. Two functions are given below.

$$f(x) = x^2 + 2x - 1$$
$$g(x) = 5x + 3$$

Find the values of x for which $f(x) = g(x)$.

3

KU	RE

10. Simplify

$$\sqrt{27} + 2\sqrt{3}.$$

2

11. Express in its simplest form

$$y^8 \times (y^3)^{-2}.$$

2

12. The graph below shows the relationship between the history and geography marks of a class of students.

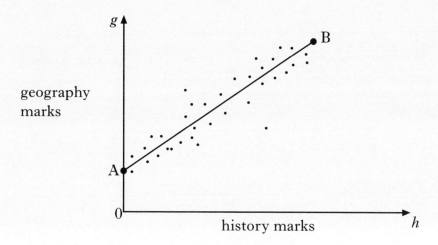

A best-fitting straight line, AB has been drawn.

Point A represents 0 marks for history and 12 marks for geography.
Point B represents 90 marks for history and 82 marks for geography.

Find the equation of the straight line AB in terms of h and g.

4

[Turn over for Question 13 on *Page six*

13. (a) 4 peaches and 3 grapefruit cost £1·30.

Write down an algebraic equation to illustrate this.

KU 1

(b) 2 peaches and 4 grapefruit cost £1·20.

Write down an algebraic equation to illustrate this.

KU 1

(c) Find the cost of 3 peaches and 2 grapefruit.

RE 4

[END OF QUESTION PAPER]

C

2500/406

NATIONAL
QUALIFICATIONS
2002

THURSDAY, 9 MAY
2.45 PM – 4.05 PM

MATHEMATICS
STANDARD GRADE
Credit Level
Paper 2

1 **You may use a calculator**.

2 Answer as many questions as you can.

3 Full credit will be given only where the solution contains appropriate working.

4 Square-ruled paper is provided.

SCOTTISH
QUALIFICATIONS
AUTHORITY

©

FORMULAE LIST

The roots of $ax^2 + bx + c = 0$ are $x = \dfrac{-b \pm \sqrt{(b^2 - 4ac)}}{2a}$

Sine rule: $\dfrac{a}{\sin A} = \dfrac{b}{\sin B} = \dfrac{c}{\sin C}$

Cosine rule: $a^2 = b^2 + c^2 - 2bc \cos A$ or $\cos A = \dfrac{b^2 + c^2 - a^2}{2bc}$

Area of a triangle: $\text{Area} = \frac{1}{2}ab \sin C$

Standard deviation: $s = \sqrt{\dfrac{\sum(x - \bar{x})^2}{n - 1}} = \sqrt{\dfrac{\sum x^2 - (\sum x)^2 / n}{n - 1}}$, where n is the sample size.

KU | RE

1. A spider weighs approximately $19{\cdot}06 \times 10^{-5}$ kilograms.

   A humming bird is 18 times heavier.

   Calculate the weight of the humming bird.

   Give your answer **in scientific notation**.

   2

2. A microwave oven is sold for £150.

   This price includes VAT at 17·5%.

   Calculate the price of the microwave oven **without** VAT.

   3

3. Solve the equation

$$2x^2 + 3x - 7 = 0.$$

   Give your answers **correct to 1 decimal place**.

   4

[Turn over

KU | RE

4. A TV signal is sent from a transmitter T, via a satellite S, to a village V, as shown in the diagram. The village is 500 kilometres from the transmitter.

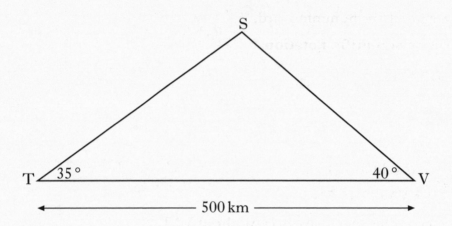

The signal is sent out at an angle of 35° and is received in the village at an angle of 40°.

Calculate the height of the satellite above the ground.

5

5. A feeding trough, 4 metres long, is prism-shaped.

The uniform cross-section is made up of a rectangle and semi-circle as shown below.

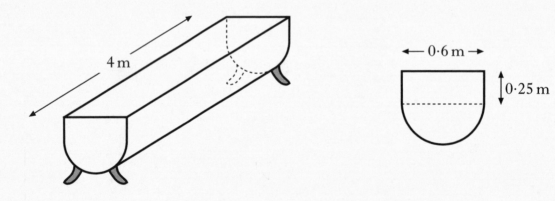

Find the volume of the trough, **correct to 2 significant figures**.

5

KU RE

6. An oil tank has a circular cross-section of radius 2·1 metres.

It is filled to a depth of 3·4 metres.

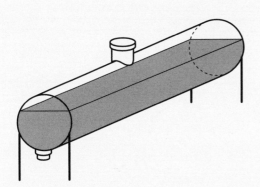 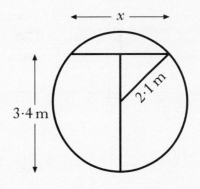

(a) Calculate x, the width in metres of the oil surface. **3**

(b) What other depth of oil would give the same surface width? **1**

7. A coffee shop blends its own coffee and sells it in one-kilogram tins.

One blend consists of two kinds of coffee, Brazilian and Colombian, in the ratio 2 : 3.

The shop has 20 kilograms of Brazilian and 25 kilograms of Colombian in stock.

What is the **maximum** number of one-kilogram tins of this blend which can be made? **3**

[Turn over

KU | R|

8. The diagram shows part of the graph of $y = \sin x°$.

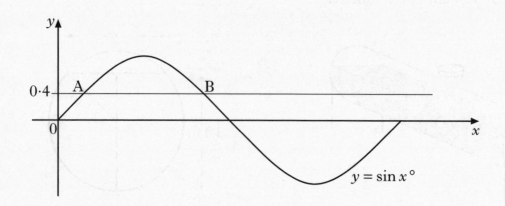

The line $y = 0·4$ is drawn and cuts the graph of $y = \sin x°$ at A and B.

Find the x-coordinates of A and B.

3

9. Esther has a new mobile phone and considers the following daily rates.

Easy Call

25 pence per minute for
the first 3 minutes

5 pence per minute **after**
the first three minutes

Green Call

40 pence per minute for
the first 2 minutes

2 pence per minute **after**
the first two minutes

(*a*) For Easy Call, find the cost of ten minutes in a day.

1

(*b*) For Easy Call, find a formula for the cost of "m" minutes in a day, $m > 3$.

1

(*c*) For Green Call, find a formula for the cost of "m" minutes in a day, $m > 2$.

1

(*d*) Green Call claims that its system is cheaper.

Find **algebraically** the least number of minutes (to the nearest minute) which must be used each day for this claim to be true.

3

KU | RE

10. A weight on the end of a string is spun in a circle on a smooth table.

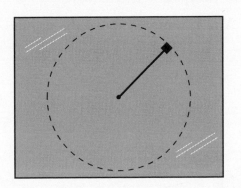

The tension, T, in the string varies directly as the square of the speed, v, and inversely as the radius, r, of the circle.

(a) Write down a formula for T in terms of v and r.

1

(b) The speed of the weight is multiplied by 3 and the radius of the string is halved.

What happens to the tension in the string?

2

11. (a) Solve the equation

$$2^n = 32.$$

1

(b) A sequence of numbers can be grouped and added together as shown.

The sum of 2 numbers: $(1 + 2) = 4 - 1$
The sum of 3 numbers: $(1 + 2 + 4) = 8 - 1$
The sum of 4 numbers: $(1 + 2 + 4 + 8) = 16 - 1$

Find a **similar** expression for the sum of 5 numbers.

1

(c) Find a formula for the sum of the first n numbers of this sequence.

2

[Turn over for Question 12 on *Page eight*

12. A metal beam, AB, is 6 metres long.

It is hinged at the top, P, of a vertical post 1 metre high.

When B touches the ground, A is 1·5 metres above the ground, as shown in Figure 1.

Figure 1

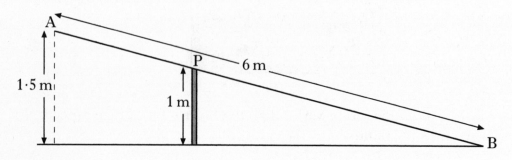

When A comes down to the ground, B rises, as shown in Figure 2.

Figure 2

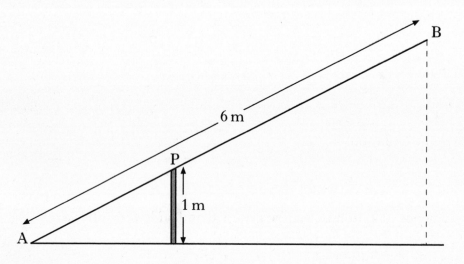

By calculating the length of AP, or otherwise, find the height of B above the ground.

Do not use a scale drawing.

5

[END OF QUESTION PAPER]

2003 CREDIT

C

2500/405

NATIONAL
QUALIFICATIONS
2003

THURSDAY, 8 MAY
1.30 PM – 2.25 PM

MATHEMATICS
STANDARD GRADE
Credit Level
Paper 1
(Non-calculator)

1 **You may NOT use a calculator**.

2 Answer as many questions as you can.

3 Full credit will be given only where the solution contains appropriate working.

4 Square-ruled paper is provided.

SCOTTISH
QUALIFICATIONS
AUTHORITY

©

FORMULAE LIST

The roots of $ax^2 + bx + c = 0$ are $x = \dfrac{-b \pm \sqrt{(b^2 - 4ac)}}{2a}$

Sine rule: $\dfrac{a}{\sin A} = \dfrac{b}{\sin B} = \dfrac{c}{\sin C}$

Cosine rule: $a^2 = b^2 + c^2 - 2bc \cos A$ or $\cos A = \dfrac{b^2 + c^2 - a^2}{2bc}$

Area of a triangle: $\text{Area} = \frac{1}{2}ab \sin C$

Standard deviation: $s = \sqrt{\dfrac{\sum(x - \bar{x})^2}{n-1}} = \sqrt{\dfrac{\sum x^2 - (\sum x)^2/n}{n-1}}$, where n is the sample size.

	KU	RE

1. Evaluate $5{\cdot}04 + 8{\cdot}4 \div 7.$ **2**

2. Evaluate $\frac{2}{7}(1\frac{3}{4}+\frac{3}{8}).$ **2**

3. Simplify $3(2x-4)-4(3x+1).$ **3**

4. $$f(x) = 7 - 4x$$

(a) Evaluate $f(-2).$ **1**

(b) Given that $f(t) = 9$, find t.   **2**

5. Factorise
$$2x^2 - 7x - 15.$$
    2

[Turn over

KU RI

6. In the diagram below, A is the point (–1, –7) and B is the point (4, 3).

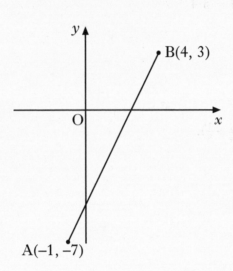

(a) Find the gradient of the line AB.

1

(b) AB cuts the y-axis at the point (0, –5).

Write down the equation of the line AB.

1

(c) The point $(3k, k)$ lies on AB.

Find the value of k.

2

7. Andrew and Doreen each book in at the Sleepwell Lodge.

(a) Andrew stays for 3 nights and has breakfast on 2 mornings.

His bill is £145.

Write down an algebraic equation to illustrate this.

1

(b) Doreen stays for 5 nights and has breakfast on 3 mornings.

Her bill is £240.

Write down an algebraic equation to illustrate this.

1

(c) Find the cost of one breakfast.

3

13. A rectangular clipboard has a triangular plastic pocket attached as shown in Figure 1.

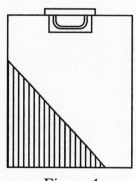

Figure 1

The pocket is attached along edges TD and DB as shown in Figure 2.

B is *x* centimetres from the corner C.

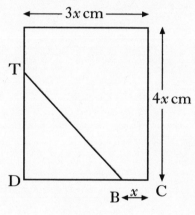

Figure 2

The length of the clipboard is 4*x* centimetres and the breadth is 3*x* centimetres.

The area of the pocket is a quarter of the area of the clipboard.

Find, in terms of *x*, the length of TD.

4

[END OF QUESTION PAPER]

[BLANK PAGE]

C

2500/406

NATIONAL
QUALIFICATIONS
2003

THURSDAY, 8 MAY
2.45 PM – 4.05 PM

MATHEMATICS
STANDARD GRADE
Credit Level
Paper 2

1 **You may use a calculator**.

2 Answer as many questions as you can.

3 Full credit will be given only where the solution contains appropriate working.

4 Square-ruled paper is provided.

SCOTTISH
QUALIFICATIONS
AUTHORITY

©

FORMULAE LIST

The roots of $ax^2 + bx + c = 0$ are $x = \dfrac{-b \pm \sqrt{(b^2 - 4ac)}}{2a}$

Sine rule: $\dfrac{a}{\sin A} = \dfrac{b}{\sin B} = \dfrac{c}{\sin C}$

Cosine rule: $a^2 = b^2 + c^2 - 2bc \cos A$ or $\cos A = \dfrac{b^2 + c^2 - a^2}{2bc}$

Area of a triangle: Area $= \frac{1}{2} ab \sin C$

Standard deviation: $s = \sqrt{\dfrac{\sum(x - \bar{x})^2}{n-1}} = \sqrt{\dfrac{\sum x^2 - (\sum x)^2 / n}{n-1}}$, where n is the sample size.

KU | RE

1. Bacteria in a test-tube increase at the rate of 0·6% per hour.

   At 12 noon, there are 5000 bacteria.

   At 3pm, how many bacteria will be present?

   Give your answer **to 3 significant figures**.

   4

2. Fiona checks out the price of a litre of milk in several shops.

   The prices in pence are:

   49   44   41   52   47   43.

   (a) Find the mean price of a litre of milk.

   1

   (b) Find the standard deviation of the prices.

   2

   (c) Fiona also checks out the price of a kilogram of sugar in the same shops and finds that the standard deviation of the prices is 2·6.

   Make one valid comparison between the two sets of prices.

   1

3. Two yachts leave from harbour H.

   Yacht A sails on a bearing of 072° for 30 kilometres and stops.

   Yacht B sails on a bearing of 140° for 50 kilometres and stops.

   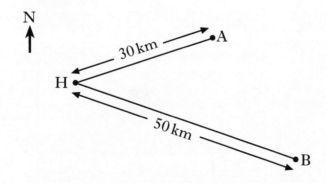

   How far apart are the two yachts when they have both stopped?

   Do not use a scale drawing.

   4

   [Turn over

KU | RE

4. A mug is in the shape of a cylinder with diameter 10 centimetres and height 14 centimetres.

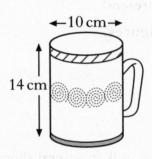

(a) Calculate the volume of the mug.

2

(b) 600 millilitres of coffee are poured in.

Calculate the depth of the coffee in the cup.

3

5. The number of diagonals, d, in a polygon with n sides is given by the formula

$$d = \frac{n(n-3)}{2}.$$

A polygon has 20 diagonals.

How many sides does it have?

4

6. In the diagram,

Angle STV = 34°

Angle VSW = 25°

Angle SVT = Angle SWV = 90°

ST = 13·1 centimetres.

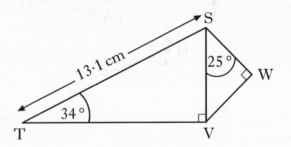

Calculate the length of SW.

4

KU | RE

7. The area of triangle ABC is 38 square centimetres.

AB is 9 centimetres and BC is 14 centimetres.

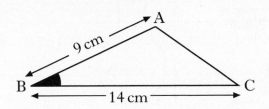

Calculate the size of the acute angle ABC.

3

8. The diagram below shows part of the graph of a quadratic function, with equation of the form $y = k(x - a)(x - b)$.

The graph cuts the y-axis at $(0, -6)$ and the x-axis at $(-1, 0)$ and $(3, 0)$.

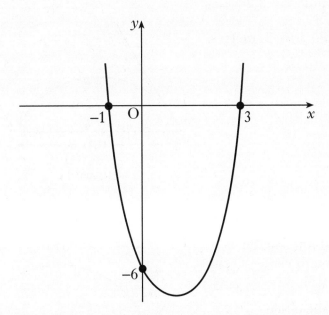

(a) Write down the values of a and b.

2

(b) Calculate the value of k.

2

(c) Find the coordinates of the minimum turning point of the function.

2

[Turn over

KU | RE

9. Two perfume bottles are mathematically similar in shape.

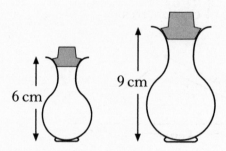

The smaller one is 6 centimetres high and holds 30 millilitres of perfume.

The larger one is 9 centimetres high.

What volume of perfume will the larger one hold?

3

10. A sheep shelter is part of a cylinder as shown in Figure 1.

It is 6 metres wide and 2 metres high.

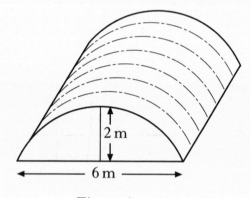

Figure 1

The cross-section of the shelter is a segment of a circle with centre O, as shown in Figure 2.

OB is the radius of the circle.

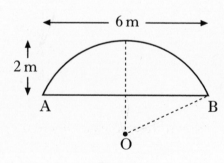

Figure 2

Calculate the length of OB.

4

11. (*a*) A driver travels from A to B, a distance of *x* kilometres, at a constant speed of 75 kilometres per hour.

Find the time taken for this journey in terms of *x*.

1

(*b*) The time for the journey from B to A is $\frac{x}{50}$ hours.

Hence calculate the driver's average speed for the whole journey.

4

[END OF QUESTION PAPER]

Pocket answer section for
SQA Standard Grade Mathematics
Credit Level "1998" to 2003

© 2003 Scottish Qualifications Authority, All Rights Reserved
Published by Leckie & Leckie Ltd, 8 Whitehill Terrace, St Andrews, Scotland, KY16 8RN
tel: 01334 475656, fax: 01334 477392, enquiries@leckieandleckie.co.uk, www.leckieandleckie.co.uk

Mathematics
Credit Level
Model Paper based on 1998 Exam
Paper 1 (Non-calculator)

1. $1 \cdot 9$

2. 65

3. 27

4. (a) 9×17

   (b) $n(2n - 1)$

5. $\dfrac{\text{BE}}{6} = \dfrac{10}{12}$

   $\text{BE} = 5 \,\text{cm}$

6. (a)

n	cf
1	33
2	50
3	59
4	67
5	70

   (b) median = 2
   $Q_1 = 1$
   $Q_3 = 3$
   S.I.R. = 1

7. (a) £68

   (b) $C = 4p + 6\,(d - 2)$

8. (a) $(2a - 3b)(2a + 3b)$

   (b) $\dfrac{1}{6x}$

   (c) $x = 0,\ 7$

9. (a) $2\sqrt{3} - 2$

   (b) $\dfrac{b^2}{b} = b$

Mathematics
Credit Level
Model Paper based on 1998 Exam
Paper 2

1. £101

2. (a) $x = 0 \cdot 75$

   (b) $\text{vol} = 7 \cdot 2 \,\text{m}^3$

3. (a) $2 \cdot 48 \,\text{m}$

   (b) $26 \cdot 72 \,\text{m}$

4. $4 \cdot 69 \,\text{m}$

5. (a) $\dfrac{1}{12}$

   (b) 25

   (c) £125

6. $16 \cdot 6 \,\text{m}$

7. $73 \cdot 4,\ 286 \cdot 6$

8. (a) $T \alpha \dfrac{S}{E}$ **OR** $T = \dfrac{kS}{E}$

   (b) 18 minutes

9. $v = 13$

10. (a) $19 \cdot 2 \,\text{m}$

    (b) $19 \,\text{m}$

11. (a) eg

7	8	9
14	15	16
21	22	23

    $(21 \times 9) - (23 \times 7) = 28$

    (b) $(n + 14)\,(n + 2) - n\,(n + 16)$
    $= n^2 + 16n + 28 - n^2 - 16n$
    $= 28$

Mathematics Credit Level Model Paper based on 1999 Exam Paper 1 (Non-calculator)

1. $4 \cdot 1$

2. 8

3. $2\frac{8}{15}$

4. $(3x + 1)(x - 2)$

5. (a) Median = 19

   (b) L = 7,   H = 44
        $Q_1 = 14$, $Q_3 = 28$

   Number of words per sentence.

   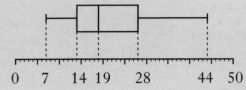

      0   7   14   19   28   44   50

6. $T = \frac{1}{2}S - 2$

7. (a) $2x + 3y = 580$

   (b) $x + y = 250$

   (c) Tickets to members = 170

8. (a) 3, 7, 10

   (b) $S_6 = -4 = 4\,(-1)$

   (c) $p+q + (p+q) + (p+2q) +$
   $(2p+3q) + (3p+5q) = 8p+12q$

   $8p+12q = 4(2p+3q)$
   $\qquad\quad = 4 \times 5^{\text{th}}$ term

9. $x < \frac{2}{3}$

10. (a) $f(4) = 81$

    (b) $x = \frac{3}{2}$

Mathematics Credit Level Model Paper based on 1999 Exam Paper 2

1. £12 000

2. $2 \cdot 366 \times 10^5 = 2 \cdot 4 \times 10^5$

3. DG = 35·5 km

4. (a) $\bar{x} = 128 \cdot 4$
   $S = 7 \cdot 9$

   (b) Older women have higher blood pressure but more variation.

5. $x = 221 \cdot 8,\ 318 \cdot 2$

6. 367·45 cm

7. $0 \cdot 45\,\text{m}^3$

8. 2·7 litres

9. 9·38 m

10. (a) 32·7 m

    (b) length of side $= \ell$.
    $2\ell^2 = (32 \cdot 7)^2$
    $\ell = 23 \cdot 122$
    $\sim\ 23\,\text{m}$

11. (a) $x + x + \text{BC} + \text{CD} = 6$
    $\qquad\qquad\qquad 2\text{BC} = 6 - 2x$
    $\qquad\qquad\qquad\ \text{BC} = 3 - x$

    (b) $x(3-x) + x(3-x-x)$
    $= 3x - x^2 + 3x - x^2 - x^2$
    $= 6x - 3x^2$

    (c) Maximum area $= 3\,\text{m}^2$
    when $x = 1$

12. (a) $d = kt^2$ **OR** $\dfrac{d}{t^2} = $ constant

(b) $d = 5t^2$

(c) distance is multiplied by 36

Mathematics Credit Level Model Paper based on 2000 Exam Paper 1 (Non-calculator)

1. 15·5

2. $\dfrac{1}{6}$

3. −24

4. (a) $(x-4)(x+4)$

(b) $\dfrac{5(2x-3)}{(2x-3)(2x+3)} = \dfrac{5}{2x+3}$

5. (a) $\dfrac{24}{50} = \dfrac{12}{25}$

(b) $\dfrac{11}{50}$

(c) $\dfrac{8}{50} = \dfrac{4}{25}$

6. $y = a + b$

7.

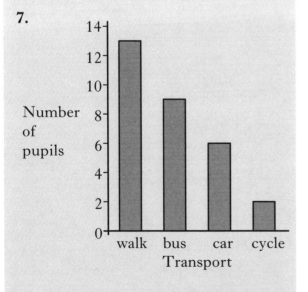

OR

Walk: $\dfrac{13}{30} \times 360 = 156°$

Bus: $\dfrac{9}{30} \times 360 = 108°$

Car: $\dfrac{6}{30} \times 360 = 72°$

Cycle: $\dfrac{2}{30} \times 360 = 24°$

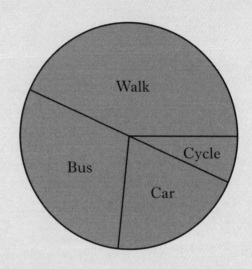

8. $y < -1$

9. (a) $a^{\frac{3}{2}} + \dfrac{1}{a^{\frac{1}{2}}}$ **OR** $a^{\frac{3}{2}} + a^{-\frac{1}{2}}$

(b) $2\sqrt{2}$

10. $V = \dfrac{3}{4}t + 5$

11. (a) $7 = 4^2 - 3^2$

(b) $19 = 10^2 - 9^2$

(c) nth odd number $= n^2 - (n-1)^2$

$= 2n - 1$

Mathematics
Credit Level
Model Paper based on
2000 Exam
Paper 2

1. 3410

2. $0 \cdot 0236 = 2 \cdot 36 \times 10^{-2}$

3. $x = 1 \cdot 2, -4 \cdot 2$

4. $\overline{x} = 158 \cdot 2$
   $s = 4 \cdot 7$

5. (a) $\ell + b = 130$
   (b) $5\ell + 8b = 770$
   (c) $\ell = 90, \quad b = 40$

6. $A = 41 \cdot 8°, 138 \cdot 2°$

7. $112 \cdot 3 \, \text{m}$

8. $d^2 \neq 22 \cdot 5^2 + 30^2$
   Frame is not rectangular

9. (a) $15 \cdot 5 \, \text{m}$
   (b) 4 am (0400 hrs)

10.
$$\begin{aligned}
\text{Vol}_{\text{space}} &= \text{Vol}_{\text{cylinder}} - \text{Vol}_{\text{vase}} \\
&= (\pi \times 6^2 \times 20) - (\tfrac{1}{2} \times 12 \times 12 \times 20) \\
&= 720\pi - 1440 \\
&= 720(\pi - 2)
\end{aligned}$$

11. (a) $1527 \cdot 2 \, \text{cm}^2$
    (b) Minimum is 45 cm.

Mathematics
Credit Level 2001
Paper 1 (Non-calculator)

1. $13 \cdot 5$

2. $8\dfrac{7}{24}$

3. $f(-5) = (-5)^2 - 3(-5)$
   $= 40$

4. $x = 3$

5. (a)
Timberplan
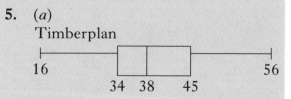

Allwoods
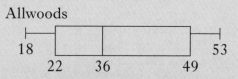

(b) **Timberplan**
Smaller Interquartile Range (or equivalent)

6. $\text{gradient} = \dfrac{\text{distance up}}{\text{distance along}}$
   $= \dfrac{t - a}{t^2 - a^2}$
   $= \dfrac{1}{t + a}$

7. (a) $\dfrac{310}{600}$ or equivalent
   (b) 70

8. (a) A $(0, -3)$
   (b) B$(-\dfrac{3}{2}, 0)$ C$(\dfrac{1}{2}, 0)$
   (c) -4

9. (a) $(7 + 1)(7^2 - 7 + 1)$
   (b) $(n + 1)(n^2 - n + 1)$
   (c) $(2p + 1)(4p^2 - 2p + 1)$

10. $\dfrac{\sqrt{72}}{24}$ or $\dfrac{6\sqrt{2}}{24}$ or $\dfrac{\sqrt{2}}{4}$

11. (a) $I = \dfrac{20}{8}$

(b) $c = 1$

(c) 2^c is a Minimum

$2^c = 1$

$I = 20$

Mathematics Credit Level 2001 Paper 2

1. $5 \cdot 256 \times 10^9$

2. (a) Mean $= 84 \cdot 3$

Standard deviation $= 1 \cdot 28$

(b) Rural prices are higher on average, and

Rural prices have a greater spread

3. Total $= £150\,907 \cdot 53$

4. (a) gradient $= m = \dfrac{(6-2)}{12-0}$

$= \dfrac{1}{3}$

intercept $= c = 2$

$y = \dfrac{1}{3}x + 2$

$3y = x + 6$

(b) $(6, 4)$

5. $7 \cdot 3$ centimetres

6. $157 \cdot 8°$

7. $x° = 184 \cdot 6°, 355 \cdot 4°$

8. $275 \cdot 7\,\text{cm}^3$

9. $R = \dfrac{kL}{d^2}$; $6 \cdot 75$ millimetres

10. (a) $107 \cdot 5°$

(b) $66 \cdot 8\,\text{cm}$

11. (a) $30 + x$

(b) $A = (30 + x)(20 + x)$

$= 600 + 30x + 20x + x^2$

$= 600 + 50x + x^2$

(c) Minimum dimensions are 35 cm and 25 cm

Mathematics Credit Level 2002 Paper 1 (Non-calculator)

1. $0 \cdot 88$

2. $1\frac{1}{2} \text{ or } \frac{3}{2}$

3. $x < 1$

4. -6

5. (a) $(p - 2q)(p + 2q)$

(b) $\dfrac{(p - 2q)(p + 2q)}{3(p + 2q)} = \dfrac{p - 2q}{3}$

6. $h = 2L + t$

7. Proof

$\cos A = \dfrac{b^2 + c^2 - a^2}{2bc}$

$= \dfrac{5^2 + 4^2 - 6^2}{2 \times 5 \times 4}$

$= \dfrac{25 + 16 - 36}{40}$

$= \dfrac{5}{40}$

$= \dfrac{1}{8}$

8. Stem + leaf diagram

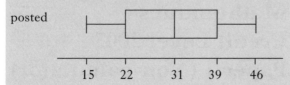

```
      posted            handed out
              5  5 │1│ 1  9
      6  5  3  2  1 │2│ 2  5  5  9
      9  7  4  3  1 │3│ 1  4  6  8
           6  6  1 │4│ 0  6  9
                  │5│ 0  0
```

Box plot

posted

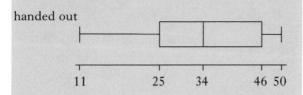

```
        15   22      31   39   46
```

handed out

```
        11        25   34      46 50
```

Bar chart

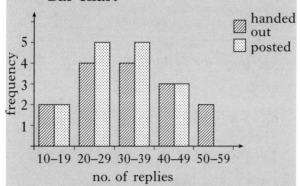

posted

no. of replies

9. $x = -1, 4$

10. $5\sqrt{3}$

11. y^2

12. $g = \dfrac{7}{9}h + 12$

13. (a) $4p + 3g = 130$

    (b) $2p + 4g = 120$ or equivalent

    (c) 92 pence or £0·92

Mathematics Credit Level 2002 Paper 2

1. $3 \cdot 43 \times 10^{-3}$ kg

2. £127·66

3. 1·3 or −2·8

4. 190·8 km

5. $1 \cdot 2 \, \text{m}^3$

6. (a) 3·3 m

    (b) 0·8 m

7. 41 one-kg tins

8. **A** 23·6°, **B** 156·4°

9. (a) 110 p

    (b) $c = 75 + 5 \, (m - 3)$

    (c) $c = 80 + 2 \, (m - 2)$

    (d) 6 minutes

10. (a) $T = \dfrac{kv^2}{r}$

    (b) Tension is multiplied by 18

11. (a) $n = 5$

    (b) $(1 + 2 + 4 + 8 + 16) = 32 - 1$

    (c) $2^n - 1$

12. 3 m

Mathematics
Credit Level 2003
Paper 1 (Non-calculator)

1. $6 \cdot 24$

2. $\frac{17}{28}$

3. $-6x - 16$

4. (a) 15

   (b) $-\frac{1}{2}$

5. $(2x + 3)(x - 5)$

6. (a) 2

   (b) $y = 2x - 5$

   (c) $k = 1$

7. (a) $3n + 2b = 145$

   (b) $5n + 3b = 240$

   (c) £5

8. (a) $\frac{1}{10}$

   (b) $\frac{1}{40}$

9. 25%

10. (a) 9

    (b) 75

11. (a) 9

    (b) n^2

    (c) $2n + 1$

12. (a) 4

    (b) $2\sqrt{3}$

13. $3x$

Mathematics
Credit Level 2003
Paper 2

1. 5090

2. (a) 46

   (b) $4 \cdot 0987$

   (c) Less variation in price of sugar than there is in milk

3. $47 \cdot 7$ km

4. (a) 1099 cm³

   (b) $7 \cdot 6$ cm

5. 8

6. $6 \cdot 6$ cm

7. $37°$

8. (a) $-1, 3$

   (b) 2

   (c) $(1, -8)$

9. $101 \cdot 25$ millilitres

10. $3 \cdot 25$ m

11. (a) $\frac{x}{75}$ hours

    (b) 60 km/h